Contents

Fast rides

A motorbike speeds away.

See it go!

Transport

Motorbikes

by Mari Schuh

Raintree is an imprint of Capstone Global Library Limited, a company incorporated in England and Wales having its registered office at 264 Banbury Road, Oxford, OX2 7DY – Registered company number: 6695582

www.raintree.co.uk
myorders@raintree.co.uk

Edited by Carrie Braulick Sheely
Designed by Lori Bye
Picture research by Wanda Winch
Production by Katy LaVigne
Originated by Capstone Global Library Limited
Printed and bound in India

ISBN 978 1 4747 4432 4 (hardback)
21 20 19 18 17
10 9 8 7 6 5 4 3 2 1

ISBN 978 1 4747 4438 6 (paperback)
22 21 20 19 18
10 9 8 7 6 5 4 3 2 1

British Library Cataloguing in Publication Data
A full catalogue record for this book is available from the British Library.

Acknowledgements
We would like to thank the following for permission to reproduce photographs: Alamy Stock Photo: Darren Kirk, 7, imageBROKER, 9, Michael Doolittle, 21 (all); Dreamstime: Papabear, 13; iStockphoto: ewg3D, 15, RapidEye, 11; Shutterstock: Anatoliy Lukich, 17, Andrey Armyagov, 8, Giovanni Cancemi, cover, Marcel Jancovic, 19, Philip Lange, 5, T. Sumaetho, zoom motion design

Every effort has been made to contact copyright holders of material reproduced in this book. Any omissions will be rectified in subsequent printings if notice is given to the publisher.

All the internet addresses (URLs) given in this book were valid at the time of going to press. However, due to the dynamic nature of the internet, some addresses may have changed, or sites may have changed or ceased to exist since publication. While the author and publisher regret any inconvenience this may cause readers, no responsibility for any such changes can be accepted by either the author or the publisher.

Parts

Start up the engine.

The engine makes power.

It makes a motorbike move.

engine

Riders steer.

They use the handlebars.

handlebars

A rider twists the throttle.

He speeds up.

Zoom!

throttle

Look ahead!

The road curves.

A rider uses the brakes.

The bike slows down.

Types

Touring motorbikes

go on long journeys.

Big tanks hold lots of fuel.

gas tank

15

Superbikes go very fast.

Riders lean over.

Dirt bikes race on dirt tracks.

They have bumpy tyres.

Some riders add parts.

They make changes.

Which bike do you like?

Glossary

brake   tool that slows down or stops a vehicle

engine   machine that makes the power needed to move something

handlebars   part of a motorbike that the rider holds on to and uses to steer

steer   move in a certain direction

throttle   lever or handle that controls the speed of an engine

Find out more

Books

Getting Around Through the Years: How Transport has Changed in Living Memory (History in Living Memory), Clare Lewis (Raintree, 2016)

Look Inside Things That Go (Usborne Look Inside) Rob Lloyd Jones (Usborne Publishing Ltd, 2013)

Machines on the Road (Machines at Work), Sian Smith (Raintree, 2014)

Motorbikes (Beginners Plus) Lisa Jane Gillespie (Usborne Publishing Ltd, 2016)

Websites

www.dkfindout.com/uk/search/transport/
Learn about different kinds of transport in the UK.

http://www.bbc.co.uk/education/clips/zmbxpv4
Discover how to design a motorbike!

Comprehension questions

1. How do riders make motorbikes speed up and slow down?

2. Look at the photos on page 21. Name a way that some motorbikes can be different from one another.

3. How are motorbikes different from bicycles? How are motorbikes similar to bicycles?

Index